WISDOM: BOOK I

✳ ✳ ✳

JARED STUART

WGA Registration 1701524
ISBN: 1500511366
ISBN-13: 9781500511364

ACKNOWLEDGMENTS

I would like to thank all of my Kabbalistic teachers (past, present and future): Abraham, Isaac, Jacob, Moses, David, Rabbi Akiva, Rabbi Bar Yochai, The Ari, Rabbi Ashlag, Rabbi Brandwein & The Berg Family. You are the heart of humanity that has maintained Light and order in this world.

I would like to thank Jesus the Christ and my entire global Catholic/Christian family who continually have me in their thoughts & prayers. Jesus is not with his family and lineage in this world. But like Rachel, who is not with her family in Machpelah, there will come a time in the future when we will all be One.

My goal throughout this life is to merge my two worlds, Kabbalah and Christianity, into one central truth. A reformatting of Christianity may take place through Kabbalah. With the Creator's help this will be the first of a series of books on spirituality in order to achieve this purpose.

TABLE OF CONTENTS

INTRODUCTION

A quest for developing a relationship with God has always seemed to consume and preoccupy me. His existence has never been something I questioned, and I am both profoundly grateful and fortunate for that. From an early age I have had an unquenchable thirst to seek and find a connection with God. I have always sought it out from every angle I could find. When I was twelve to thirteen years of age I remember asking the Creator to give me Wisdom. I believe my exact words were, "Please God make me a wise person". I did not know what exactly that would entail, but I realized by that age that I needed God's Presence in my life. I remember God reaching out to me as I began to just have conversations with Him. It is God who found me through this time. I did not find Him, He really found me. An over-whelming feeling of certainty overtook me through my early connections with God, and I knew the Creator existed and was Present among me. I consider these early years, which to this day are vivid in my mind, as the initiation of my faith in God. Around this time I also found *The Bible* and opened it to the book of *Proverbs, Chapter 3*. As I read *Proverbs* I remember the Creator, or what felt like a covering Presence around me, clearly conveying that my prayers were heard.

By age sixteen I had read *The Bible* cover to cover, and eventually found myself at Pepperdine University finishing a Bachelor's in Religion and a Master's in Ministry. I received amazing information through a university education, but it was head knowledge not life experience. I realized toward the end of my Master's degree that I could not work for any one religion or denomination. Toward the completion of my graduate work I found Kabbalah. Kabbalah is known as Jewish mysticism, but it is so much more than a mystical understanding of Judaism. It is actually a connection to the Infinite Light that has created all of existence. This Light is the foundation of all spiritual understanding including

Judaism. The concepts of Kabbalah are fortunately available to all individuals regardless of age, religion, ethnicity, gender and orientation. For the past ten years I have worked in the business world during the day, and studied Kabbalah in the evening. This time has produced a myriad of experiences that have allowed my heart to catch up with my head. All the academic knowledge I attained has integrated with experience, and allowed me to develop a spiritual awareness and compassion that I did not have before.

One of the greatest gifts the study of Kabbalah has given me is clarity into my Christian understandings. I was raised and am a practicing Catholic, and though I thought I had answers to faith-related questions prior to studying Kabbalah, I really did not. Over the past decade I have continually encountered the paradox of how Kabbalistic teachings (which on the exterior after 2,000 years do not resemble modern Christianity) could somehow provide me answers about a relationship with Jesus the Christ. Kabbalah has indelibly provided me essential answers. The process of studying Kabbalah has completely transformed my understanding of Christianity. I have had to allow dogmatic belief systems to be released, and come to the realization that Kabbalah does not have to conform to Christianity. Rather it is Christianity that may eventually conform to key concepts found in Kabbalah. Kabbalah after all precedes Christianity. There is therefore a reformatting that could take place. Through the study of Kabbalah a Christian would be able to transcend 2,000 years of historic alterations, and realize the essence of Christianity. Conversely, those who come from a Kabbalistic/Jewish tradition can find purpose in this book, too. The teachings of Jesus Christ (and the Holy Spirit that flows through a relationship with Him) and the practice of Judaism are by no means mutually exclusive.

Spiritual transformation is a challenging process, and reading my writings will not be easy; but I think the reward is well worth it. The purpose of my writings is to share my own faith journey and realizations. Through my writings I hope you find guidance as well as a connection to an authentic form of spirituality. I pray you are blessed through reading this book. I know I am blessed to share my insights with you. Please feel free to share your thoughts and reflections with me at bookofwisdom@earthlink.net.

CHAPTER 1

SEED & MANIFESTATION

Wisdom is seed and manifestation all wrapped up in the Present Now. It is beginning and end united together. It is the transcendence of time. Some would call it experience, and if we were viewing it from a time bound point of view this would be correct. But from outside of time experience plays no role in the creation or attainment of Wisdom, because by Its very nature Wisdom is outside of time; and yet imminent throughout time.

How do we plead with the Holy One to bestow upon us His most precious stone; this being Wisdom? And why should we desire It? First, we must recognize how limited we are in our human experience. We are time bound entities at present who have forgotten why we are limited in the first place. We are limited because we lack His Presence through Wisdom. We should desire the opportunity to remember what the purpose of our experience happens to be.

How challenging would it be to go on a journey without plotting one's destination? We would know where we are beginning, but we would not know our final destination. By not knowing the destination it kind of devalues the beginning before the experience even begins. But even if we have a clear idea of the destination we will not have any idea of how to connect points A and B. This is where Wisdom comes into play. Not only does it provide purpose for our journey, but it also provides guidance along the way. Wisdom sees outside of time and gives purpose to our process because It helped form it in the beginning. Wisdom stands there waiting for us to call upon It in order to assist us in what we desire; that being ultimate fulfillment. It sees in essence our beginning and our end, and the infinite and highest roads to journey in order to get there.

What is the first choice we can make to bring into our experience a relationship with Wisdom? In order to form a relationship with Wisdom we must recognize where It comes from; that being the One Holy God. The Holy One created the heavens and the earth through Wisdom. What does this mean? It means the Holy One used His own energy to manifest everything from beginning to end all at one time. This energy has left a residue that permeates this physical experience. This residue is Wisdom and It is imprinted into everything that exists within our physical reality. It is thus eternity transcending into our human experience.

Wisdom is in Itself a paradox because how can that which is transcendent of time also be moving through time? It is a paradox to apprehend but possibly not comprehend. It is sufficient to understand that Wisdom is God's way of communicating with us through our time bound experience. Once we realize what Wisdom is, that being the essence of the Holy One among us, we can both recognize where Wisdom comes from and why it is imperative that we plead for It.

CHAPTER 2

ATTAINMENT

When it is said by King David that a "holy and reverential fear of the LORD is the beginning of all Wisdom", what is being said is that we should take it upon ourselves to fearfully remember how necessary it is to desire Wisdom throughout our days; and therefore, plead with the Holy One to provide us with It in order to successfully fulfill our journey. Who would want to be here indefinitely? Would one want to run a marathon without a finish line? Indeed no. So pleading for Wisdom is a wise choice, and recognizing where It originates is even wiser.

Wisdom begins in the heart and not in the head. Why? Because only through the eyes of the heart can the soul convey within the human experience the incomprehensible connection between seed and manifestation. Our journey is thought out and completed in its perfection at inception; and this inception begins at the seed level. Thus, manifestation has already occurred as far as Wisdom is concerned. There is no duplicity with Wisdom. It knows beginning from end, and the best way of getting there.

In order to attain a true relationship with Wisdom we must relinquish the need to think our way through life according to our own understanding. Rather we must know our way through this journey by allowing Wisdom to guide our way. This is a knowing that transcends our own understanding, and precludes logic. In order to ascertain the Infinite within this human experience we must relinquish our need to control and deduce our own outcomes. We must choose to relinquish and release everything. This is what is meant when Jesus Christ prayed, "Not my will but Thy will be done." Human will begins in the head, but Divine will enters through the heart. We must allow

Divine will to encompass our desires, and drive us because that is what will bring us fulfillment.

When we are in the driver's seat instead of the Holy One our lives slowly go off course. Eventually, we are so off course that we do not even realize what our purpose is for why we are here. Our intellects rationalize how far off course we are in order to stay in control. Yet the heart which connects us to Wisdom knows how far off course we truly are. It does not think. It knows; and the dissonance within these two aspects of ourselves, the head and the heart, is a disquieting discontent that we all have experienced.

The heart is guided by Wisdom. Wisdom is the essence of the Holy One among us. It resides within everything that exists including trees, rocks, and yes even our own DNA. Some may call this a pantheistic idea. In truth though God exists everywhere. He is also whole and sovereign beyond what we can conceive. God is among us everywhere, and also whole beyond us. God's fingerprints are among and throughout us. These fingerprints are God's manifested essence that we know as Wisdom. We are constantly called and reminded of these embedded sparks of Light throughout every waking moment. The heart knows this reality. It resides in this truth. This truth is constant, it is not dualistically and emotively high and low. It is unwavering in its certainty of what true reality happens to be. When we choose Wisdom in our lives we choose to be guided by this heart felt certainty, and it can never lead us anywhere but toward our highest and most fulfilling destination.

Some would say the heart is sentimental and therefore not to be trusted. In reality, the heart is oneness and certainty. The head or human ego opposes this certainty and oneness. It desires us to logic our way through life based on our own understanding. It convinces us that we have all the answers, and deduces answers that we do not yet have based on limited information. The ego ultimately cannot be trusted because it dualistically leads us toward untruthful outcomes. When we follow the heart, which is the gateway to the soul and our connection to Wisdom, we may not have all the answers but we can be certain in our highest outcome. When Wisdom is allowed to guide us we connect to our highest fulfillment. We sense in every fiber of our being why we are here and where we are going.

When we are guided by the heart which permeates every cell of our being we begin to form a relationship with the Creator who formed us. Why? Because the Holy One's fingerprints reside in every cell of our body. He is there, within us and among us. Our egos convince us otherwise but we silently know the truth. We are already complete right now. A new career, a better education, new clothes or new relationships will not add to this completion. We are already complete right now, we just do not recognize it yet. We do not realize that our fulfillment has already begun on a seed level, and the manifestation of this fulfillment is Present among us. We are surrounded by the fingerprints of God. These fingerprints, which is Wisdom, is among us waiting to be felt and admired.

Wake up completed one. Your fulfillment knocks quietly at the doorway of your heart. Like a gentleman He is standing at the doorway of your life waiting for you to answer the call. God is patiently waiting for you to recognize the Voice that spoke you into existence. How wonderful it will be when each of us recognizes this Voice and opens the door of our hearts to this call; and we begin our amazing journey home. In reality, we have already arrived. We just do not know it yet.

CHAPTER 3

ON THE WAY HOME

B ecause Wisdom transcends time it can see simultaneously both seed and manifestation. As we travel on our human journey we encounter trials and difficulties. We encounter these difficulties after they have already manifested. We in essence become the effect of what has unfavorably manifested. But there is a better way. By connecting to Wisdom we can see the paths we might travel and view all circumstances from the seed level. We can choose right now the thoughts, speech and actions that will simultaneously manifest into our highest fulfillment. By aligning with Wisdom we align with our highest destiny.

It is the life God desires for us to have. Only through connecting with Wisdom and making God present in our lives can we have true control over everything. And here lies the paradox. How can we have control by letting go of control? How can we make sure we are headed in the right direction by getting out of the driver's seat? It is an interesting realization, and one that each of us must realize on our own. No sermon or book can cause this realization because it is an awakening moment that each of us has to realize through experience. And that is why we are here. We are here to have such experiences and consequent realizations.

God gave each one of us free will to drive our own lives; to draw conclusions and make decisions as we see fit. The human race has been doing this since the dawn of time. After this amount of time it just feels right to continue on this way. Yet humanity has never been in a worse state. The ego would have us believe sovereignty over our lives would lead toward a more perfect state, but in actuality it is leading toward a manifestation of destruction. What is the solution? The solution is to get out of the driver's seat. But when we do this we feel out of control. We look over from the passenger's seat and see no one driving the car. We must know that Wisdom is there. The invisible One's fingerprints are there on the wheel. They are turning the wheel on a seed level in ways we cannot even begin to realize. They are manifesting outcomes for us in the future that are for our highest good. They are avoiding road blocks that we did not even know existed. We must lose control in order to gain control. We must let go of the steering wheel and allow the fingerprints of God to steer us through this journey of life. It is why we are here. It is why we are having our human experience.

The purpose of the human experience is to give us an opportunity to earn a relationship with the Creator through exercising our trust in His reality, and not our own. The Holy One gave us free will so that we could experience everything like God experiences. After all, we are made in the image of our Creator. This is what we desire. We have an innate desire to be like our Creator. It is for this reason that we desire to be in the driver's seat. And this is our lifelong dilemma. The only true free will we have is to return our free will back to the Creator, and build a trusting relationship with the Creator in order to fulfill why we were given free will in the first place. The only reason we were given free will is because we asked for it in order to experience a relationship with God. Our free will is most completely fulfilled when we choose a true relationship and relinquish control back to the Creator. Once God's fingerprints are back on the wheel and not our own we have begun a real relationship, and actually have realized true control over our destinies. It is a paradox that does not make sense if processed through the ego or head, and because it is so paradoxical the human race continues down the path of impending destruction. But if we allow Wisdom to find Its way into our hearts and we let go of a need to understand by our own standards, life begins to take meaning. We become whole like the Creator.

CHAPTER 4

ONE INTELLIGENCE

O ur hearts are analogous to a bodily gateway that leads to our soul. There is a Divine spark in each of us that connects us to the Creator regardless of age, gender, ethnicity and religion. The heart speaks the language of spiritual understanding that encompasses every cell that exists and is alive in our being. It is cellular intelligence that makes up who we are. This intelligence knows beginning from end because Wisdom is deeply embedded in its origins. This intelligence has no beginning and no end. God's fingerprints are around us wrapping us up in His infinite arms.

We awaken to this reality when we begin to trust the intelligence that permeates through our heart and into the essence of who we are. In actuality, it is not that we are connecting to an organ known as the heart, though this organ is a physical manifestation and representation of this intelligence; but rather we are connecting to that region of our body that Wisdom can be awakened and experienced through. Some have said through the centuries that our bodies cannot be trusted, and that God can only be experienced through rational thought. This is true if by connecting to the heart one is denoting a connection to animalistic, emotive desires and egotistical, self-centered reactions. If this is the case then rational thinking can be of benefit. Conversely, if connecting to the body denotes allowing human emotion and feelings to dictate self-centered habits and actions, then the rational mind can be beneficial. And so religion in all its debaucheries has actually served quite useful because it has used the human rational mind to stave off human whimsical selfishness through the institution of rational doctrine and dogma. But ultimately religion has not created a solution for the human condition. It has maintained order but it has not brought ultimate fulfillment into the human experience. This can only be brought about by each of us choosing to reconnect to that which created us; and in each of us realizing why we are here in the first place. In order for anyone to make this reconnection we have to realize that God is right now among us, and Heaven is right now and yet beyond. We are all currently connected through the reality of our existence. Wisdom resides in the present and so do we. This makes us all one with the One Creator of us all. The intelligence in me is the intelligence in you. When I heal you, I heal me. When I hurt you, I hurt me. It is an intelligence that unifies and transcends borders, religion and any egotistical imaginations. When one nation bombs another, that nation bombs itself. It is an intelligence that is simultaneously in a single cell and everywhere all at once.

There is only one fingerprint, the fingerprint of the One God. Understanding our individual and collective intelligence is what creates order, not religious dogma. Religion can stave and dissuade external chaos, but ultimately it cannot effectuate everlasting fulfillment. It will never change the human condition because an intellectual understanding of one's own existence ultimately cannot connect one to this intelligence. God's intelligence is connected to by coming into an awareness that what exists in me is exactly what exists in you, regardless of externalities; and that therefore, we are one as the Creator is One. Regardless of what our dogmatic desires rationalize, at the end of the day I am you and you are me. Destroying the fingerprints in you is effectively destroying the fingerprints in me. It is a present reality that our ego constantly wants us to forget. And this is why God is really so easy to connect to, and yet why a connection is so elusively and perceivably challenging to sustain. He could not make Himself any more accessible than by imbedding His intelligence and essence in every aspect of our existence. And yet the individual, rational mind convinces each of us daily that this intelligence does not exist.

How do we indelibly remember who we truly are? It is very simple. We choose to recognize on a very tangible level that God's Wisdom exists, that His fingerprints are everywhere. We experience the cellular intelligence in ourselves, and as we become increasingly aware of it we begin to sense it in others. As we sense it in others we recognize that it transcends our ego's rationalized barriers of religion, ethnicity, orientation and gender. We experience the discomfort that God exists beyond our barriers and we embrace this uncomfortable truth. We allow the rational, dogmatic mind to be transformed through our realization of One Intelligence, and we consequently begin to transcend what the head or the rational mind can offer us. We thank dogmatic religion and governmental systems for giving us what it can offer us and we begin to open ourselves up to a new existence. Thus we afford sacred space for the Infinite to exist and operate among us in a new way. The room we allow must be Infinite and without conditions from now on in order for this Infinite Intelligence to be in the driver's seat.

CHAPTER 5

REAL FULFILLMENT

R eligion is analogous to chemotherapy. We have all taken it because we all have the same cancer: our ego. Chemotherapy kills the bad but it also kills the good along with it. Eventually the bad continues to grow because the root cause of what is manifesting the dis-ease is not addressed, and eventually there is no more good left to sustain the system. The body dies and the soul returns to the Creator to complete its experience in a new way. Religion conquers our free will and sterilizes society, but at a cost. The cost is our most precious commodity: eternal fulfillment. Fulfillment is the ultimate completion of our experience. It is the complete relinquishing of our control and our choice of unification with the Creator. It is the realization of why it is in our own best interest to get out of the driver's seat and hand our lives back to the Creator. When we hand over our free will we find our fulfillment.

Through religion we are white washed on the outside and left on the inside in a state of disheartening dissonance. We have a desire for approval from an unattainable externality which can never be realized. Religion propagates an illusion that all is well, but just under the surface lies a dissatisfaction that no externality can truly mask. And it is irrelevant which religion we are talking about. There is only One God and this Creator has revealed Himself among many cultures and epochs. The revelation is not the problem, our filtering of this Infinite Light in order to encapsulate It into a controllable, finite formula is the dilemma. The Infinite can never be deduced into the finite. Religion seeks to do this and this is where religion ultimately fails. Our rational, finite egos endlessly struggle to wrap and contain the Infinite, and in the areas that are beyond our comprehension, we

choose to draw conclusions in order to fill in the blanks. Out of our assumptions dogma is birthed. When dogma reaches its complete maturity intolerance is formed, and the rest can be read about in history books.

How does the cycle end? We end the cycle by inviting Wisdom into our lives. By recognizing that the Creator's Infinite essence is imparted like a residue of Light throughout all that exists we can in return find our interconnectedness with everything. We choose to relinquish our ego to a new reality that has lasting benefits. By doing so we release religion's control over our lives while still connecting to the Infinite essence that religion has been trying to impart to us all along. We do not lose our individual identities by recognizing our true fulfillment. However we are created is who we should continue to be. It is exactly how the Creator would like us to stay. The Infinite resides to bring fulfillment in each of us regardless of the finite distinctions that give us our individuality. We should never alter ourselves or others. This is the Creator's work not our own. The Infinite's Voice is constantly reverberating through each of us saying,

"Experience fulfillment in Oneness. Come as you are. I am complete in you." And when we hear that resounding echo in our being we reply, "I am One and Complete as I am a reflection of the Infinite." It is this completion and fulfillment that transcends religion. This is not relativism. This is reality. We are all One. We are all finite vessels coming from one Infinite Light. What distinguishes us is not a reflection of any flaws in our finite makeup, rather our differences are a cosmic reflection of the One's Infinite Creativity. And why would we think it would be otherwise? How could an Infinite Force be anything other than Infinitely Creative? And if the One is Infinitely Creative would that not create a diversity that is beyond what we could imagine as acceptable? We need to redefine within ourselves what we deem allowable in the human experience. What we redefine as allowable needs to go even beyond what we can define as tolerable. It needs to include what we cannot perceive as permissible. As long as "Love Thy Neighbor" is the litmus test for what goes on in our lives, then everything is permissible. When we create new definitions for our lives we create a fulfillment that infuses into the very existence of our experience. We are born again into a new experience. This is a reality that sees Light and commonality in everything.

CHAPTER 6

TO RECEIVE

J esus Christ speaks in the book of *Matthew 11:10* that, "Wisdom is proved right in Her actions." Wisdom is often referred to in the feminine pronoun. This is because Wisdom is the remnant of the Creator's handiwork which resides in our physical existence. It is our road map that leads us home and into endless fulfillment. In Kabbalah there are ten dimensions known as emanations. In Hebrew these emanations or dimensions are known as "Sefirot". The physical world in which we inhabit in Hebrew is known as the "Nukva", and also known as the dimension of "Malchut". It is the tenth and final dimension, and is thought to have no Light of its own. It is a dimension that only receives Light which has been filtered down through the higher nine dimensions. Like a vessel this dimension can only receive. Similar to Wisdom, we also refer to Malchut in the feminine. And we refer to the Light, the force of the Creator that gives this dimension life and sustenance, in the masculine. In actuality, the Creator is both masculine and feminine in energy. As it states in *Genesis 1:27*, "So God created man in His own image, in the image of God He created him; male and female He created them." The feminine side of God is reflected through Wisdom. It is this essence of God that resides among us. Wisdom is proved right in Her actions in that even though It is encapsulated by time and space, this Infinite Oneness understands beginning from end.

The real question is how an aspect of the Infinite can be trapped into our finite existence? This is a question beyond comprehension. What we can know is that God is real and present in this dimension we call life. He has entered the game of life, and has a stake in its outcome. His highest outcome is that each of us develops a relationship with Him. It is the sole reason He created our souls and this human experience. In order for us to accomplish this goal and win the game, however, we need to know the rules. The rules are outlined and codified in *The Bible*, and revealed through the holy Kabbalistic biblical commentary known as *The Zohar*. Through the ages these rules have been memorized by the most brilliant of theological minds who in spite of their brilliance have failed to succeed in transforming our world. It can be concluded that the reason for their failure is due to a pursuit of life from an egotistical understanding instead of a heart dependent on Wisdom. They sought to win the game of life and cross the finish line in a state of self adequacy and sovereignty. They sought a life of perfection and justification. These individuals thought as they crossed the finish line that they would hear from the Creator "welcome home". Instead they heard "go start over". What did these brilliant minds not understand, and why is Wisdom proved right in requesting these souls, who by all apparent standards are righteous, to start again? Wisdom is correct because She understands that the game of life is not about attaining perfection, but rather it is about developing a right relationship with the One who designed the game; and also about a right relationship with those other beings who are playing along side us, and sometimes against us.

This whole existence is about relationships. The rest is details. In order to form right relationships we must love. We must invest and offer the best of ourselves in life the same way God does. Our fingerprints need to be seen and felt in others around us, and visa versa. Investment is an inconvenient necessity in this game we call life because it necessitates that we hand over everything we have to the game. We cannot hold anything back. Jesus Christ comments in *Matthew 6:21*, "Where your treasure is, there your heart will be also." We may fool ourselves along the way but God cannot be fooled because He is among us. He knows what we treasure and whether our hearts are seeking true treasure. True treasure can only be found by chasing a true relationship with the Creator and with others along side us. We must chase it like we chase gold and honor because this is where our true success is found.

In order to attain true success we must come to the greatest realization which is that the highest attainable life is to "Love God" and "Love Neighbor". It is what we know to be the only true rule of life. Only through a redefinition of what true treasure happens to be can we hope to succeed in this game of life. We can choose to play this game indefinitely. The Creator can wait an eternity for us to come to our conclusions. But do we want to wait that long? Wisdom is proved right in Her actions. God is right in allowing us as many opportunities as needed on this Wheel of Life in order to come to the conclusion of what we are here to accomplish. Every one of us can choose now to finish the race by choosing right relationships which are founded on "Love God" and "Love Neighbor" or we can continue endlessly on the Wheel of Life by choosing egotistical, rational alternatives. If we choose the latter we can rest assured the game will continue here or elsewhere, and it will not end until the right choices are decided. This is not an exposition on reincarnation, though Lurianic Kabbalah certainly has a very detailed theological understanding of reincarnation. It is an affirmation of the pre-existence and resurrection of the soul which is eternal like the Creator who formed it.

Who is our "Neighbor"? Our neighbor is every other human being along side us on this Wheel of Life. Regardless of race, gender, religion, orientation, our neighbor is every human being we encounter. We are called to love every human without exception. There is no justification or cause as far as God is concerned that amends this rule of life. To find a cause or justification, however rational, is to not understand why we are here. Wisdom will keep us on the Wheel of Life until our justifications are exhausted. Is it not easier to just realize that we are all One? Be of good courage lest we think another is more righteous than us. They might have just been on the Wheel a bit longer than us. There is none righteous except the Creator who grants us continual grace and perpetual opportunities to transform as *2 Corinthians 3:18* writes, "from glory to glory".

CHAPTER 7

SEEKING & FINDING

King Solomon writes in the book of *Proverbs* how we should seek Wisdom and Understanding. If the Creator is already among us why are we seeking It? It is because our ego prevents us from knowing we are already complete through His Presence. Why would the Creator create a world of illusion that would allow our egos to prevent us from a knowledge of completion? It is actually we ourselves according to Kabbalah that requested this egotistical illusion. In the fall of the Garden of Eden, Adam and Eve, who are metaphorical of all human souls that exist, requested this illusion. When they ate from the Tree of Knowledge of Good and Evil *The Bible* is metaphorically revealing that humankind has requested to go through a relational evolution with the Creator in order to earn a relationship with Him. The Creator is completely beneficent and overflowing in a desire to overwhelm us with His Presence. But it is we who have chosen to push this relationship with the Creator away. How many of us have had someone in our lives, whether it be a parent or a spouse, who gave endlessly without in return receiving back from us? Perhaps we did not even have the maturity or capacity to return what we received. How did this make us feel? Instead of making us feel whole and complete it actually made us feel empty and humiliated. The reason is because as humans we want to feel that we receive in life what we have earned. When we feel that we have earned what we have there is value in what is received.

The dilemma in our relationship with the Creator is how can we return anything to an Entity who already is whole and has everything? How can we share with The Holy One who is all sharing and not in need of receiving anything? We cannot and so the illusion of ego has to transpire. The fall of Adam and Eve is not a mistake on the part of the human race. It is part of the natural spiritual evolution of how humanity is developing a mature and conscious relationship with the Creator. The Creator desires to know us. *The Bible* uses the phrase "to know" in a very special way. When it writes in *Genesis 4:1*, "And Adam knew Eve" it is referring to a sexual connection between man and woman. But this knowledge between male and female energies also has a deeper connotation. Knowledge or knowing is synonymous with Wisdom. Wisdom resides among us and seeks to know us as well, but Its existence is hidden from us. Why? Because we have asked it to be this way. We ourselves have asked to be incomplete so that we can earn our connection to the Creator; and so that we can share in creating our own fulfillment. The Creator is already complete. He is waiting for us to complete ourselves through entering into a relationship with Him. Are we ready to plead for Wisdom and seek to be known by the Creator? He stands at the doorway of our hearts waiting for an invitation to come in. Our connection with the Creator though requires our initiation.

To think we can offer the Creator anything is a misnomer. The only way we can give back to the Creator is to allow Him to take over our lives. We have to give back the sovereignty that we initially requested. This is the only gift we can offer the Creator and consequently the greatest gift we can give. When we do this it creates a circuitry in ourselves that is next to invincible. We become complete and made whole like the Creator is. It is analogous to Adam finding his soul mate, and Eve becoming complete in her purpose.

God is both male and female energy. He created us in His image. The Creator is both pure Light and pure Vessel. Male energy is outward and sharing. The physical male traits are a manifestation of this energy. (Note: matter is just condensed Light or Energy). Female energy is inward and receiving, and the female physical traits also reflect the condensed energy that manifests these traits. When male and female know each other in the physical they are in the spiritual realm creating a circuitry that reflects the wholeness of the Creator. It is for this reason that sex is so powerful, and why it should be preserved and honored with complete holiness. The sexual union is one of the greatest reflections of spiritual wholeness. Sexuality, which is the reflection of the male and female energy in physical reality, is beautiful and overwhelmingly powerful. It is meant to be this way because it is a physical expression of our eternal completeness. God's essence is expressed in this expression of humanity because His consciousness created our DNA. We cannot escape from a relationship with God any more than we can escape from a relationship with each other. And so we return to the inevitable dilemma of seeking after that which we innately already know. We already have an innate connection with God through our very existence. But we must choose to understand and receive this connection.

When it comes to a relationship with God we are the Vessel. The Creator is the Light. Our nature and role is to receive the Light. There is no greater gift we can give the Creator than to request that this Light come into our lives, and to receive It through appreciation. We connect to the Creator by making ourselves open to receiving His Presence. Perhaps it is easier for women to understand this Creator/human connection because it more mirrors their relationship and role in the physical reality. Women have an easier time overcoming the illusory ego because they understand more easily on an energy level how to receive. For this reason many see women as actually more spiritually evolved than men even though they have held fewer spiritual roles of authority throughout history. The concept of receiving strikes at the heart of the male ego. We should evaluate women's role in spirituality. By creating a balance of energy in the physical reality we can create a much more balanced spiritual connection globally. It begins though with an understanding of who we are and how our Creator connects with us.

CHAPTER 8

A KING'S HEART

The traits of the wise are a reflection of Wisdom. King Solomon's reflections in the books of *Proverbs, Song of Solomon and Ecclesiastes*, and King David's reflections in *Psalms*, are a portrayal of what it means to be wise. In these books we receive instructions on how to enter into a relationship with Wisdom. The LORD's handiwork is completed in us through an integration of these writings into our lives. They are writings that appear to be so pragmatic and simple. They appear to be commonsensical information that any one of us would know, and that is because we do. Our very DNA is founded on these writings.

The cellular intelligence of our being is very aware of everything contained in them.

On a cellular level we understand who we are. It is for this reason that David's and Solomon's writings appear so pragmatic and basic. They are also however concurrently elusive to live out in our day to day lives due to our ego. The ego is that part of ourselves that causes us to second guess what we know. What we know is not a knowledge founded on human intellect or rational thinking, but on a certainty of who we are and why we are here.

The Creator created us to experience not just mere existence, but an expansive awareness and oneness with the Creator and each other. The only way to connect to this awareness is through a connection to Wisdom. The Kings' writings open a doorway for us to connect to our true selves, and to create a roadmap home. Even more importantly the writings not only guide us home, but they also converge us on a Present path that forges an eternal relationship with the Creator; which is the reason for the journey in the first place. Let's begin a journey into the Kings' Writings.

Proverb 21:1 writes, "The king's heart is a stream of water in the hand of the LORD." What Wisdom is teaching us through this passage is how to lead our lives. A king represents leadership. We ourselves must govern our own lives so that we are fluid and flexible throughout the challenges we face. We are responsible for every action we do. But more importantly we are accountable for every thought and feeling we have, as well as every word we speak and action we commit. The passage goes on to state, "Every way of a man is right in his own eyes, but the LORD weighs the heart." It is the inner recesses of us that the Creator is working on. He wants us to live lives that are fluid inside and out. He wants resonance in our thoughts, feelings, speech and actions. In order to attain this resonance we have to be aware of the Kabbalistic understanding of water. In Kabbalah, physical elements and properties are a manifestation of spiritual energy. They are condensed Light visible and attainable to us through the five senses. In Kabbalah, water represents the spiritual attribute of mercy, or in Hebrew "Chesed". The waters of mercy flow from the upper emanations and cover us from the judgment and justice we most probably have brought upon ourselves through our own past thought, speech and actions. Mercy is surrounding us so that time is expanded between cause and effect. Mercy is an energy force that affords us an extension of time between the effect of what we caused. Through a connection to Wisdom we become conscious of our causes, and therefore responsibly empowered to create a reality at the seed level. We in essence become the cause rather than the effect.

For every action there is an equal and opposite reaction according to the law of Newtonian physics. Time is the distance between our actions and their effects. One might ask why would we as humans need a time delay between our actions and their results? The reason is so that we would truly have free will. Without the opportunity to forget why we are experiencing what we are going through, we would not have the free will to have made the choice in the first place. If pain immediately resulted from choices we have made, we would likely not make these choices. We would be outside of time like the angels and clearly see the eternal connection between cause and effect. But the Creator designed a world for us humans where great distances of time are often formed between our actions and effects. The One did this for two primary reasons. The first reason is so that we would have the choice to be like God. In other words, so that we would choose unity, unconditional oneness and balance with ourselves and all that exists. The second reason is so that we would have a time delay to recognize that when we hurt another human we ultimately hurt ourselves. This realization should out of self interest cause us to repent.

What does it mean to repent? In Hebrew the translation is "Teshuvah". We do not think of teshuvah as remorse or feeling guilty, though those might be temporary emotions felt through taking responsibility for everything we think, speak and do. The word teshuvah actually means to turn in the opposite direction. Teshuvah in this sense is not an emotion as much as it is an action. God affords us mercy in order to grant us time to repent, or act in a new way. We should constantly plead with the Creator to show us every day how we have disconnected from the Light. Whenever we realize that we have acted wrongly we should then feel the pain we have caused, and in turn release it. The worst mistake we can make is to stay in the pain after we have made the choice of teshuvah. This is not a solution. The true solution is to fully experience the pain and emotion, and then to release it. As we release it we make the commitment to act in a new way in the present and future. It is our opposite action that creates renewal and allows us a new present.

Each one of us are rulers of our domain. We are fully responsible for the gift of life afforded to us. We can think of ourselves as kings and queens. A king's power resides in the responsibility he assumes in governing correctly all that is entrusted to him. A true king of his domain understands how important repentance is in his life. He also realizes that he must function daily through mercy because he recognizes how much mercy he requires and has been afforded. His heart is in constant reliance on the Creator. He recognizes how easily his thoughts, speech and actions could go off course, and so he surrounds himself with the waters of mercy, and allows that fluidity to flow through him.

A king is like a living stream that flows through the hand of the Creator. The hand represents that which fashions and forms. We must allow the Creator to fashion and form us. In order for this to happen we must be fluid and flexible. It is our rigidity that disallows God to create in us the best version of ourselves. In our rightness we lose our fluidity. We must be quick to afford mercy to ourselves and others, because there are times when even if we are right we are really wrong. To remain fluid we must always have open ears to hear the quiet whisper of the LORD which calls us to repentance. When we are keen to hear and quick to repent life becomes fluid, and peace resides within us and all of our relationships. We become an extension of living water and God becomes our Quiet Advocate in life.

We are the Creator's creations that flow easily through the palm of His hand, and this fluidity allows us to rule over our own destinies. When we flow freely through Him, and He through us, life becomes easier. Challenging times will arise and apparent injustices will come our way, but we will know that this world is governed by cause and effect. Through living in a perpetual state of repentance we can avert many future effects from our past causes, and alter the course of our individual and collective futures. It is the most powerful way to rule the world. We rule the world by ruling ourselves. Teshuvah and mercy can alter everything because the Creator has created a world that He wants to see succeed. He recognizes that we will disconnect from our highest destiny through life; in fact God realizes it is inevitable. It is part of being human and finding our way home. This is why He created mercy in the first place. It is to give us time to re-create our highest destiny. We need to search our hearts constantly and hear His quiet Voice. It is right there waiting to be heard like an advocate right beside us. When we do this we create unity and oneness within ourselves and others. We become the highest version of ourselves and live out our best destinies which He foreknew for us. Our hearts become light and renewed, and we see ourselves as God sees us because we become a reflection of The One.

CHAPTER 9

WORSHIP

Why does King David write in *Psalm 27:8*, "My heart said of You, 'Go worship Him.' So I came to worship You, LORD."? Why was it David's heart that spoke to David? The reason is because the Creator's Light speaks though the heart of man. Only the heart of man can grasp the Infinite Wisdom of God. Those who try to attain it through ego will never be spoken to clearly. And if God does answer someone operating egotistically according to his own understanding, the rational mind will doubt whatever answer is received. The answers God gives us throughout our journey are always simple, and usually not what we would expect. As the Prophet *Isaiah* writes of God in 55:8-9, "My thoughts are not your thoughts, and My ways are not your ways." Who can understand the vastness of Infinite Thought? Can the mind of man? Of course it cannot, and yet it continues to try. Through our own understanding and conclusions religion forms and divisions ensue. The prospect of actually trying to understand the thoughts of God should terrify us. We should tremble at the thought of it not because we serve a terrifying God, but rather because a right relationship with the Creator should be done with an understanding of His vastness, not the illusory proficiency of our own capacities.

In order to have any relationship we need to know how the other person thinks, how he reacts, what his expectations of the relationship are, and what he values. While the Infinite Light Force can never be thought of as a person, the Light is a Presence that has a clear Essence and Identity. When we read about the prophets' and the kings' experiences with connecting to this Identity we begin to form how our own approach should also be. In our own finite way we should seek to understand this Essence with our whole heart, strength and will; and not with an egotistical, dogmatic, intellectual understanding.

Approaching the Creator is known as worship. In order to worship we must approach the Light correctly. As King David writes in *Psalm 111:10,* "Wisdom begins with a holy, reverential awe for the LORD; those who obey His orders have good understanding. He should be praised forever." What is David conveying to us about his connection with the Creator? David is speaking to our human condition which he shared in. Our ego resides in its own sovereignty. It thinks it is sufficient in and of itself. In order to enter into the Presence of God, however, we need to let go of our sovereignty and who we think we are. We need to release all thoughts about ourselves and others, and allow His Presence to redefine what we conceive to be correct. Our worship is made complete when we allow the Light of His Presence to transform our understanding. God's thoughts, however ineffable, need to take precedence over our egotistical will, desires and conclusions. A heart of gratitude is formed as we realize that we are connecting to an Infinite Force that is transforming us into His Image, rather than we becoming a part of what we perceive to be God according to our own sovereign understanding. We do not approach worship with what we think we can offer, instead we allow ourselves to be redefined through the One who recalibrates us into what we are at the seed level. This connection is a transformation that returns us to a reality that is incomprehensible to our ego. It is beyond our own understanding of who we think we are and what we perceive reality to be. We praise God to return to our true nature, a nature that resonates with the Wisdom that continually creates us.

King David writes in *Psalm 111:1*, "Praise the LORD. I will thank the LORD with all my heart in the meeting of His good people." David understood the secret of forming and maintaining a right relationship with God. It is said that he had such holy, reverential awe for the Creator that he could not get a full night's sleep. This reverence for the Creator would awaken him in the night. What does this mean? What was really waking David? It was his heart's realization of how much his life was reliant on the Creator, and his understanding of where his life force derived from.

Out of this genuine realization came an intense gratitude and connection to the Creator. David awoke because he realized that the breath he just took could have been his last. How many of us have this kind of consciousness? Most of us take a breath and think that we deserve it, and those breaths that follow are rightfully ours as well. Our egos convince us of our sovereignty. David however knew the frailty of his own sovereignty, and as a result had a holy awe for the Creator who provided him his next breath of life. It was David's consciousness that created for him a full and complete life.

We need to be more like King David if we want to understand God's Thoughts and not just our own. David actually is quite a good role model for many of us today. He was a man who was very acquainted with the ways of this world. He did not have the cleanest track record through-out his life. In this regard he was ahead of his time. David did many transgressions that according to even today's standards would be considered not the holiest of actions. In this sense we should consider David not the best role model. But the Wisdom of God sees him otherwise. God says in the book of the prophet *Samuel 13:14*, that "David is a man after My own heart." What did David understand that transformed him into a man whose heart resembles the Heart of the Creator? David profoundly understood that repentance, not perfection, leads to a closer proximity with the Creator. David would awake in the night not only because the last breath he just took could have been his last, but because in all reality it actually should have been his last breath. David knew at all times how far away he was from the Creator. He was constantly trying to narrow this distance, not justify it. He praised the Creator because he needed God's attention to narrow this distance. His praise and worship came from a recognition of dependence. Our worship often comes from a negotiation to retain our own sovereignty. It is out of David's understanding of his own human condition that God reveals that David, among all men throughout history, has a heart that reflects and resonates with the Creator.

We serve a renewing God. The Creator is constantly wanting to restore us like He did David. The Creator wants to heal everything that is broken in us. But first we like David have to relinquish the absurdity of our own sovereignty. We have to get out of the driver's seat and allow God to determine our reality. In order to do this we have to tell our rational, egotistical mind to take a permanent vacation. It knows not what the Creator values. We have to relinquish our sovereignty and our understanding of who we think we are and what we think we deserve. We have to understand that we do not even deserve the next breath we are about to take. Everything is a gift from the Creator who created it. We are owed nothing but the opportunity to recognize who afforded us this gift, and to receive this gift with gratitude and praise. When we have such an understanding we find a right relationship with the Creator, and Wisdom is then clearly expressed in hearts of fulfillment.

CHAPTER 10

RENEWAL

King David writes in *Psalm 51:10*, "Create in me a clean heart God, and renew a right spirit within me." We often conclude that in order to be spiritual we need to religiously engage God, and there is truth in this. But the reality is in order to be truly spiritual we need to realize that it is actually the Creator who has already gotten involved with us. In order to have an awareness of God's Presence in our lives we first need to plead for Wisdom. We need to have an understanding that God is Present in every circumstance and situation. Out of this awareness we can then prepare ourselves for His Presence which is already among us. It is similar to knowing someone is in a room though not knowing exactly where this person is. We feel a Presence even though we cannot see who it is. David first experienced the Presence of the Creator. He then had the Wisdom to understand that his life had to be transformed in order to accommodate this Presence. David did not clean himself up and then ask God to enter his life. This is unfortunately not the way it works. David recognized his human condition by comparing himself to the Presence he knew was about him. He then sought transformation through realigning his heart through re-pentance. But without Wisdom first residing in David he would not have had the capacity to recognize this Divine Presence in the first place. In this regard it really is the Creator who forms a relationship with us first, and not we who first initiate this relationship. In order to understand the Creator is present we must first plead for Wisdom to see beyond our own sovereignty.

God is a gentleman and He is constantly knocking at the door of our hearts, and asking to be invited in. He desires to enter our worlds in order to clean out our hearts and renew a right spirit in us. In order for us to hear this knocking, which often times is ever so silent, we have to know that His Presence exists. If we want a right relationship with the Creator it must be on God's terms, and not our own. God comes knocking just as we are; unclean and unrenewed. When we hear the call we should wisely answer the door immediately. We cannot in our self-sufficiency ignore the call until we think we are clean enough to answer. The truth is we will never be clean enough and we will have missed the opportunity of connection. It is God's Presence that cleans and renews us, and makes us whole. It is always the Creator that renews, and it is always according to His order and timing. God's grace is sufficient. We just need to answer the door when the Creator calls.

In order to hear the knock we need to have a heart of dependency like David. David flooded his mind with silence and worship; which seem to be mutually exclusive, but in actuality they are not. He chose not to rely on his own egotistical self sufficiency, but rather on his certainty that the Creator could alone transform his brokenness.

How many of us approach God like David? How many of us do not? How many of us, instead, tell the Creator how righteous we are, and when the Holy One has the right to enter our lives? A truly spiritual being knows the Creator is Present, and depends on that Presence to reveal what needs to change, and then to consequently effectuate that transformation. Most of us today measure ourselves by our own standards. The Creator is another acquaintance that we schedule into our lives. We answer His call when it is convenient for us. We push aside His calling Voice when It conflicts with what we truly worship; that often times being ourselves. We are all guilty and need transformation in this area.

The door of our heart that the Creator is constantly knocking on is in itself an illusion because the truth is that God is everywhere. He is already on both sides of the door, and also in parts of us that we are not even aware exist yet. He is not asking to be let in, He is asking for us to acknowledge that He is already Present. This prospect both terrifies and annoys us, and so we create doors of distance in order for the Creator not to breach our boundaries. We feel incredulous to His Invisible Presence, and so in our sovereignty we ignore the Creator. It is almost embarrassing to admit our behavior. Like a perfect gentleman, however, the Creator allows us our timeline. He silently waits until circumstances change and schedules are eventually shifted, and a call of need is made by us. He then pretends to enter our domain in order to assist us with the aftermath of our own self-sufficiency. And when we have everything cleaned up and back in order, and even sometimes when we do not, we show the Creator the door and thank Him for answering the call. He allows us the illusion that He has exited our world much the same way that He illusively entered, but in truth He has been among us the entire time. It can be no other way. He is everywhere. Always has been, always will be. It is we who need to come to the reality that we are never alone, not God who needs to alter His eternal Presence among us.

The Creator can only leave us to the extent that we choose to no longer feel or recognize His Presence. There are some who because of traumas in life do choose to shut God out. It is either too painful to think that the Creator could be present in such pain, or they cannot comprehend how the Creator could have permitted such a transgression. We should never judge another's experience because we cannot understand their own Wheel of Life; nor should we underestimate why another human needs to walk through the experience they are going through. Regardless of circumstance and situation, we cannot forget that the Creator is Present. We can indict Him, we can even divorce ourselves from His existence, but He is still Present. That can be a comfort or it can be a nagging annoyance. He allows us our freedom and timeline to choose what our relationship will be with Him. We have an eternity and His position in wanting to be Present in our lives never changes. He never changes. We hopefully do change. Our transformation however begins by acknowledging His Presence.

CHAPTER 11

REAL RICHES

roverb 3:9-10 writes, "Honor the LORD with your wealth and with the first fruits of all your produce. Then your barns will be filled with plenty, and your vats will be bursting with wine." Kabbalistically, the idea of wealth transcends monetary riches. Wealth is the energy that encompasses and surrounds that which we value. Wealth includes good health, rewarding relationships, financial abundance and a healthy environment. In all of these areas though it is the energy or Light that resounds within them that is what is of most value. A dollar or any form of currency can be devalued to the point where it is only paper if the energy it embodies is not respected. A loved one can become an enemy if the relationship is not honored and sanctified. Health can be deteriorated if the system is not understood and respected.

We live in a world today that often times respects the exterior or surface of what we see, and not the energy behind it. Materialism has run so rampant that it has blinded us to what actually sustains us. Wisdom is calling us back to the Source. It is calling us to realize that abundance is found through an appreciation in what we value, and a respect for everything we currently have. We can only keep what we value. We can only value what we appreciate. We can only really appreciate what we realize is a gift from the Light.

Everything we have is a gift from the Light. We are given the opportunity to earn it and manifest it, but we should never confuse earnership with ownership. We own nothing except our relationship with the Creator, and even this is a gift. We are only a vessel for Light; nothing more. Our role as a vessel is to manifest abundance with appreciation. If abundance is not flowing through us, it is not because Light does not want to give us every- thing. It is because we have short circuited our capacity to receive through a lack of appreciation of what we have, or we have misused in the past what we received. When we misuse wealth it creates a short circuit in our vessel. The pipelines of sustenance get blocked and we are unable to receive the endless Light that exists. It is our respon- sibility to clean out these blockages and re-connect those channels of sustenance. We do this through repentance which re-connects us to abundance.

Blockages can occur on an individual level and also on a collective level. Sometimes individual souls come together as families because they share the same block- ages. Kabbalah refers to this as "like attracts like". We attract those who share our same blockages, or those who can assist us in removing our blockages so that we can re- open our channels of sustenance. It is no accident what region, country, culture and family we are born into. We ourselves choose our reality in order to return us to abun- dance. Every circumstance and interaction is exactly what we asked for in this life. Acknowledging this is our first step in removing our blockages to abundance.

A spiritual individual is an abundant soul who takes responsibility for everything. It is someone who proactively chooses to do his/her spiritual work. Spiritual work is not sitting on a mountain top meditating in silence and isolation, though such retreats can be occasionally beneficial. Spiritual work is re-opening our connections to the Light so that we can receive all abundance and then share it freely. Spirituality takes work, but it is the ultimate reason why we are here. Spirituality requires us to look at all the ways we are poverty stricken and not behaving as a sharing human. Kabbalah takes it one step further in that it requires us to look at why we are currently poverty stricken and in lack; whether that be financially, emotionally or physically. It requires us to seek out our past disconnections from the Light, and our present egotistical agendas and habits; and then to take responsibility for them and our present condition. There is no one to blame in Kabbalah including ourselves because all roads eventually lead home. Wisdom however provides us with the quickest and least invasive way to get there. When we seek out the Light of Wisdom, and then live out that Wisdom through the Light of Sharing, we are guaranteed success in all areas of life. The life that is created may not be what we could have possibly imagined because it has the capacity to be so much greater than what we can conceive.

Wisdom will grant us the insight to attain everything but there is a cost. The cost is us choosing to do the non-stop, daily spiritual work that we came here to do. It requires us every second to take full responsibility for everything in our current self movie; the debt, the failed relationships, the unrewarding career, and then to rejoice in it. We must reside in full acceptance of our present reality and exist in a state of unwavering happiness and certainty that where we are is exactly where we need to be. It is our happiness and certainty that draws down the Wisdom we need to transform our nature in order to attain our next level. And it is the Wisdom that we consequently receive that gives Light to our actions of sharing. It is the action of sharing that causes the transformation that creates abundance. But it all begins with happiness.

This is a state of happiness that is a choice not a whimsical emotion, and we paradoxically choose it because we have certainty that where we are at is exactly where we need to be in order to go to our next level. Only through a certainty that we are right where we need to be can we go to our next level, and happiness is a reflection and a catalyst of this certainty. What is our next level? It is that next frontier where we grow in a closer connection with Light and endless fulfillment.

We know our affinity with the Creator has gone to its next level when we start to resonate the attributes of Light. What are these attributes? First and foremost, it is a sharing nature. The Light's consciousness is that of sharing. When we have a consciousness of sharing we know we have an affinity with Light. When we have an affinity with Light, abundance in all areas of life naturally follows.

True spirituality is simple and never easy. It is constant work and it never ends. From the day we are born until the day we exit this world we must consciously choose to become beings of unconditional sharing and forgiveness.

Our egos will consistently try to convince us that what we have is ours. The ego will also convince us that what we have we own, and that everything ultimately will not be returned to the Creator. It is the greatest deception we can fall prey to, and without a spiritual awareness deception will happen. It needs to be a constant reminder that all we have is a gift, and that we have been given the opportunity to earn what we have in order to then responsibly share it. When we understand that we are simply vessels to channel Light, and that our spiritual work is to re-create channels for abundance to flow through, then abundance and success become a by-product of a happy, well-lived life, instead of a means to an end.

1 Timothy 6:10 writes, "For the love of money is the root of all evil." Many know this passage and throughout history it has been misunderstood. It is the love of money, not money itself, that is the root of all evil. Money in this passage represents idol worship. The worship of idols is more than putting one's trust for sustenance in a carved wooden object like the ancients once did. For us today idol worship is much more elusive. It includes placing one's certainty for survival and fulfillment in a career, a relationship, or one's own faculties and talents. In essence, an idol is anything that replaces the Light in our lives. Evil is what ensues from this idolatry. In Kabbalah, evil is nothing more than a disconnection from the Light which is the Source of all abundance. When we are disconnected from Light, darkness floods into our lives and this emptiness creates depression, jealousies, and all kinds of chaos. In actuality, darkness cannot flood in because darkness is not an entity in and of itself. It is nothing more than an absence of Light. Evil or darkness is not the opposite of Light, it is the absence of Light. When we place our trust in idols instead of the Light of the Creator we consequently push abundance away from our lives.

Why would we choose idols instead of Light? Because it is an easier choice. It is easier to trust in what we can see with our five senses, and it is also easier to control and have self-sovereignty through this choice. It also allows for short term gratification and the appearance of success. Our egos constantly coerce us into trusting idols instead of the Light behind that physicality that gives it value. When this happens a devaluation occurs to physicality. We are living in a very uncertain and sorrowful age because of egotism. Devaluation is occurring throughout our world. It is occurring to our monetary currencies, to our food supply, to our environment, and to our relationships to the Creator, ourselves and one another. Chaos is ensuing as a result of Light being extracted from that which we are currently valuing. This devaluation and inflation is subtle, but it is becoming increasing impactful. When a critical amount of Light has been extracted from our physicality the effects will be devastating.

The irony is that there is more spiritual awareness among us today, yet there is less genuine spiritual work being done than ever before. Yes religion abounds, but spiritual work is not being done. The result is an eventual devaluation of life itself. It is occurring at all levels of society; from politicians, to entertainment professionals, to all of us sitting comfortably in our homes and taking in the audio and video information that fuels this devaluation. No one in particular is at fault because we are all at fault and responsible. We are all in the same boat, and millions of holes are simultaneously being drilled into the boat through our collective choices.

What is the solution? The solution is to see past the illusion of idolatry. We have to seek out our idols and throw them away. Each and every one of us needs to start self transformation through daily spiritual work. There is no easy way out of the situation our world finds itself in. There is no easy quick fix. Starting to love again the Source of what we value, instead of the material manifestation of it, is our only choice. It is not going to be easy. It will be the most challenging choice we all will have to make, but ultimately it is the only viable option.

In order to avert an implosion of materialism we need to begin to infuse Light back into that which we currently value, and awaken a true appreciation for the Source that sustains life through a return to genuine spirituality. If we choose otherwise a collapse will occur that no one can fathom. The collapse will affect all spectrums of life. The monetary supply will be inflated and of no value. The food supply and livestock, which has been treated with little to no dignity, will begin to spread pandemic disease. The environment will unleash torrents of irreparable catastrophic chaos. And our children will not have the common sense to honor the lives of their own parents who gave them life because they will have no capacity or vessel to comprehend why life should be valued. It is our collective calling to end this dilution and begin condensing Light into every particle of matter that we are entrusted with. This must begin now.

We must wake up to the call of why we are here. We are here to love that which should be loved, that being the Light of the Creator which is what sustains this world. It calls out constantly to us to return to our Source. We simply need to wake up to Its call and know It exists right now. It is a simple choice. When we all choose to live for the Source that sustains existence, and to live lives of unconditional sharing, abundance will flow endlessly into our individual and collective lives. The result if chosen will be so much greater than anything we could ever imagine.

CHAPTER 12

NO PAIN NO GAIN

P *salm 1:5-6* writes, "Therefore the wicked will not stand in the judgment, nor sinners in the congregation of the righteousness." There are humans who choose a spiritual process in this life, and to those around them it appears as if their life is cursed, when in reality their life is endlessly blessed. Conversely there are others who appear to be blessed in this world but who are actually not. Often what appears to be true according to our physical five senses is not really the case.

There are two ways to correct the soul. In Kabbalah, we refer to these two ways as "Ashrei" (I happily thank you God for allowing this to happen) or "Oy Vey" (Oh God why is this happening to me). Ashrei is the road of the righteous. It is the path of a proactive, spiritual transformation for the soul. Oy vey is the road for individuals who reactively choose to let life happen to them. The righteous are those who take full responsibility for their life movie, and they participate in this movie in full appreciation and acceptance because they know that the Creator is in their presence despite what their five senses are telling them. The righteous accept everything with certainty and allow every circumstance to provide them with an opportunity to forge a deeper relationship with the Creator. They understand that through their certainty they are unified with the surrounding Light. They have a trust that any pain they experience has a purpose and that it provides them with an opportunity to more intimately cleave their soul to the Creator. Through their proactive, conscious choice to accept pain they understand an affinity is formed with the Light, and through this affinity they become more like the essence of the Creator; that being a vessel of sharing and mercy.

It often seems that the more righteous an individual is the more pain that person endures. We can reflect on the lives of Jesus the Christ, Rabbi Akiva and Rabbi Shimon Bar Yochai. Jesus Christ was crucified on a cross by the Romans, Rabbi Akiva was skinned alive by the Romans, and Rabbi Bar Yochai had to hide in a cave for approximately thirteen years buried in dirt in order to escape execution by the Romans so that he could complete his teachings. Yet all three men indelibly transformed our world, and all three endured intense pain throughout their lifetimes.

It is a paradox that the righteous will stand in the world to come while the wicked will eventually fall. But the Light is a paradox. It is God who guides the path of the righteous, and He exists throughout the pain that they endure. The righteous are able to stand only because the Creator is invisibly present among the pain. One reason the Creator is present is because the righteous have invited Him to be present. The righteous understand the reason for pain, that being an opportunity to cleave to the Creator in order to create an affinity and likeness with His essence. As a result, the pain is neither something to be avoided nor averted. It is also not something to be sought out, it is merely a part of the inevitable process of allowing the Creator to guide their paths. To place one's trust in the certainty that the Creator is present is to submit to the Creator's sovereignty. To understand sovereignty is to know that God has designed the absolute best possible life for each of us. It is our job just to live it out with appreciation. We are not here to redesign the lives we are given, we are here to embrace everything our lives have to offer in order to transform our natures into His essence.

If we are in this world then we have spiritual work to do in order to further develop our affinity with the Light. There are aspects of ourselves that do not yet reflect the nature and essence of the Creator. The righteous understand this and therefore embrace the opportunity to further their affinity through proactive transformation. They see pain as an opportunity to transform, and they have certainty that God will not allow a circumstance that they cannot be sustained through. The wicked however do not even understand their own existence, and so they live in a world of oy veh. There is no Creator that these individuals acknowledge to exist; their only reality is their physical five senses. Everything for the wicked is a random occurrence and so pain is to be avoided, and pleasure is to be maximized. God is a notion that can be entertained religiously for the sake of familial and communal closeness, but for the wicked God is not a force to place one's existence in. For such individuals reality begins at birth and ends at death, and their thoughts, speech and actions revolve around such a linear reality. What causes certain humans to become wicked is not the Creator Himself, but rather their own uncertainty in the Creator's existence. They are unable to stand in judgment in the world to come because they have avoided all the pain and circumstances granted to them throughout their lives which have been intended to prepare them for eternity. The reason they avoid it is because eternity is not yet a reality.

We are here to build an affinity with the Light. We have taken human form to develop thought patterns and ways of interacting that embody sharing and unconditional love. The pain that we experience in this world prepares us for eternity. It imbues our vessels with the ability to earn the Light of Wisdom and Mercy, which is what we need in order to reside amongst the Creator throughout everlasting eternity. As we endure the pain and hardship in this life we need to know that the Creator is present through it. As we grow in this certainty we allow the Light to transform us into new versions of ourselves. This life becomes a workout for the life to come. Our future is bright when we realize that what we experience between birth and death is a fraction of reality. Our role in this world is to constantly remind ourselves not to define who we are according to what our egos value (fame, fortune, recognition) but to rather remember to constantly live out lives that transcend this present, physical illusion. It is a complete illusion to base one's values and priorities on what the five senses deem as real. We are all susceptible to this illusion, even the righteous. This is why the righteous invite life to play out as it is intended to be. They accept pain because they know it is a sure way to break this present illusion. Pain is an opportunity to realize true reality; a reality founded on eternal priorities, not materialistic agendas.

We as spiritual beings can have vast material possessions, and many righteous souls such as Abraham the
Patriarch have been quite wealthy, but the righteous neither see these possessions as an end to the means, nor
do they define their worth and value by them. They see
material possessions as riches that have been entrusted
to them in order to wisely share. They are in this respect
possessed by the Creator and not by their possessions.
The righteous are able to stand in confidence in the world
to come because they have not given into the illusion of
physicality. The Creator knows the way of the righteous
because the righteous made time in this world to form an
affinity with the Light. They allowed the pain of life to
build a relationship of trust and certainty with the Creator,
and through this relationship the righteous become one in
form and substance with the Creator's attributes of sharing
and unconditional love. We can learn from the righteous
when we make it a priority in our lives to do likewise.

CHAPTER 13

HUMILITY

James 4:10 writes, "Humble yourself in the sight of the LORD and He will lift you up." Likewise, *Proverbs 3:6* writes, "Acknowledge the LORD in all your ways and He will make your paths straight." To walk humbly is to have certainty that the Creator is among us throughout any and all circumstances. It is to know that God is among us and sees everything. We therefore watch our steps and where our paths cross because the Creator is ever before us. We also are reverent in our thoughts, speech and actions because we know the Creator is within us.

Humility is a state of being. It is a consciousness of mercy that results in a behavior and form that is pleasing to the Creator. We know true humility when we experience it in ourselves and in others. We also know false humility when we see it. The ego can imitate humility in order to adapt and conform to social norms and religious agendas, but genuine humility begins with an acknowledgment that the Creator is among us and within us. It is God alone we answer to. The whole world can reject us for numerous reasons, but if we humbly know the Creator is guiding us through our process then this is how true humility begins. Conversely, the whole world could revere us and we could put on an air of humility, and yet the Creator could be nowhere near the path we are on. It is analogous to a parable of two men examining their lives. The first man is a very pious man esteemed by his community. He regularly attends church/synagogue and wears the proper clothing attire. He is mere inches from the Creator's throne and yet his back is completely turned to the Light. The second man is miles away from the Creator because of actions he has done throughout life, but his eyes are transfixed on the Creator. He understands and acknowledges the distance between him and God, and is racing to bridge that distance. He will not take his eyes off of the Light until he finds his way home. Who is closer to God? The answer is the second man because he clearly understands his dependence on the Light of the Creator.

To walk humbly is to not have an agenda. We have to relinquish what we think we know, and allow a desire for the Light of God to be our only true agenda. Only then will we be able to create lives that bring us ever closer to the Light. We have to relinquish everything our egos desire: "which church/synagogue should I belong to?", "what friends should I associate with?", "what career will bring the greatest notoriety and fortune?", "what neighborhood will reflect the highest social stature?". If we want to be constantly face to face with God our only agenda must be "how can I create an affinity with You?". This is true humility. A life pleasing to God is one that simply asks the Creator, "How can I help?", and understands that every gift and talent is given to us for the purpose of sharing and manifesting Light in this world.

The Bible says that Moses was a humble man. Many theologians have contemplated on what this means. The first forty years of Moses' life he lived among Egyptians. The next forty years of his life he lived among Midianites. It was not until he was approximately eighty years old that he was reunited with his own people the Israelites. Moses most likely did not know the religious and social ways of his own people though he resembled them in likeness and form. He likely did not know how to dress like them, or how to even speak and pray the way the Israelites did at that time. But Moses knew how to talk with God and listen to His Voice. Moses simply knew how to obey, and this is why he was usable by the Creator. We can learn prayer books, dress/attire, and various social customs, but if we do not have a simple relationship with the Light we will never find our way home.

Moses spent most of his life in a desert wilderness. In spite of this environment his agenda was simple: unity with the Light. It is this kind of unity that disintegrates ego; and when ego is gone we are left with real wholeness and completeness. It is what we all desire, but we have to let go and let it happen. We acknowledge the Creator by letting go. It's simple. Letting go is humbly allowing the day to happen, and having certainty that this is bringing unification between us and the Light. Everything else is secondary to creating this unification. Moses had his own people ready to stone him throughout his life. It did not deter him. He knew his Source and why he was on this earth. Moses' life revolved around a simple relationship with God. He allowed daily circumstances to be governed around this relationship. The circumstances did not move him. They did not detract from this relationship because his ego had been disintegrated through the simplicity of humility. We however most of the time allow our circumstances to dictate our relationship with the Creator. We are moved by our circumstances and our relationship with the Creator is compromised. Our egos solidify not disintegrate when this happens. Before we know it we are miles away from the Light.

We may not recognize it but distance forms once our agendas supersede our simple daily connection to the Creator. Like the parable we can be religiously and socially close in proximity with the Creator and yet quickly find ourselves miles away from Him without knowing it. Before we realize it we have forgotten who we are and have become shells of acceptability in proper attire. The loneliest place to be is alone among a crowd. When we have everything except a connection with the Creator we are truly alone. There is no greater emptiness and the only remedy is to humble ourselves and acknowledge that our relationship with the Creator supersedes anything and everything else. This does not necessarily mean returning to a church/synagogue. What it means is to reconnect to God by simply talking and listening to Him. It means just walking with Him daily like Moses, and allowing our lives to become the miraculous versions of existence that they were meant to become.

Moses used to reside in his own tent outside the encampment of the Israelites. Some probably thought he was lonely. On the contrary, he was fulfilled because he was truly not alone. When we recognize and acknowledge who walks among us, that being the Creator of everything, life takes on a brilliance that no circumstance can alter. We begin to experience miracles in the simplest of circumstances. In addition, we are also afforded the certainty and strength to walk through any trials because we know who is walking among us. This is not a realization that a church/synagogue can teach us though if we want to expand our spiritual consciousness it does help to be around like minded individuals. The certainty that the Creator is among us is a realization that can only come through experience. The relationship is there for each and every one of us to form. By our very gift of existence and awareness it is there for us. We only need to desire to create it. If we do choose a daily connection we can be certain that circumstances will arise to challenge that relationship with the Light. But know those circumstances are going to come regardless. Each choice to maintain a certainty in the Light and choosing not to be moved by circumstances that arise will build an affinity with the Creator; and that is what we came here to do. That affinity or likeness of essence is what expands our spiritual consciousness. We call this in Kabbalah an expansion of our vessel. When our vessel or soul is expanded we begin to naturally create miracles in our daily lives. Though extraordinary to others they become ordinary to us because we become One with the Creator. This is each individual's purpose for being here.

We are here to walk simply and serve God first. There can be no agenda in life except this simple reality. This relationship is our greatest treasure. An agenda to manifest money, fame, a large house, or even a beautiful family for ourselves can create circumstances that can compete with our relationship with the Creator. Every one of us if we are honest with ourselves know this truth; and the times in our lives when we chose our circumstantial idols over the Light can be recalled, in fact they really can never be forgotten until we repent and transform. The amazing truth about the Creator is it is never too late to get back on track and come home. The gradual distancing from the Light is a slippery slope and before we know it we find ourselves miles away from the Creator. Like the second man in the parable we realize our condition and ask ourselves how we got so far away from our Source so quickly. Like a current that can carry someone so far away from shore we can feel the insurmountable fear of getting back to shore. But God is simple. He wants us home. No matter how far we have drifted He desires immediate proximity with each of us. We just need to set our eyes on His infinite Light and start bridging the distance; He will complete the rest.

It is a simple walk. It only becomes complicated when we confuse it with our agendas. Difficulties come to every one of us through health, relationships and career; they are unavoidable. In fact they are necessary. Often times it is only through our difficulties that we fortify our certainty and affinity. It is in the quiet moments as well as the challenging ones that a relationship with God is formed. We should therefore never run from our circumstances. They are our crosses to bear. They are what stirs God's heart to be in our lives and make Himself known to us. In reality He is here all the time, but it is we who forget Him, not the other way around, during the good times. This is why difficulty is necessary for some more than others. It often times is the only occasion we develop our relationship with God. Don't worry, He does not mind. He likely is amused by it. Like a loving Father He thinks of us constantly and looks forward to us coming home. But the beautiful reality about this Father is we already are home because He is right now among each of us.

CONCLUSION

MESSIAH COME

The Prophet *Daniel* writes, "But the wise shall understand. They who are wise shall shine like the brightness of the firmaments." Wisdom comes from Light. It infuses into us through our consciousness. It is a cellular infusion that takes place inside out. The Light is a spark within everything that is self contained and expansive. When we allow our consciousness to be expanded by Light, life is activated in every cell of our being and we shine outwardly and unconditionally. It is we who choose life, not God who chooses it for us. God has already chosen it for us by His very nature.

The Light is invisible and everywhere. We as sentient beings activate Light within us through conscious intent. It is Wisdom that reveals to us that Light is among us. Light seeks to be manifested through us. This manifestation cannot come outside in. It must express inside out. We shine like the firmaments when our certainty activates our awareness that Light is Present now, and we understand our existence when we recognize our sole purpose is just to shine.

We are the vessels the Light created to express Itself. We exist to express Light. Knowing our nature is vital to understanding our purpose. Many would think it is opposite, they approach the quest for meaning in life without realizing their true nature. It is our nature that gives meaning to our purpose. Our nature is to be a conduit of Light. It is to be the vessel for the Creator to express Itself to the world. When we move within our real nature we find an endless reservoir of life and naturally find our purpose. Ultimately our purpose is to reflect the nature of God. It is to have resonance with the Light of the Creator. What better way to activate that purpose than to allow the

Creator to work through our lives? We just need to let go of the steering wheel and allow Light to create us.

We need to be open to the Light's Presence. This is where Wisdom comes in to assist. Wisdom gives us understanding to know what our nature truly is. In the day to day realities of life our egos can override our true sense of purpose. Our egos can convince us that we are someone other than who we really are. We reside in a world of physicality. It has no Light of its own. It lives only to receive. It is a vessel like we are. The ego convinces us in this dimension that what we receive is outside of ourselves. This is part of the egotistical illusion that we accepted upon ourselves when we chose to become human and reside in this physical existence. Our egos play on our need to receive, and our need to receive is a reality. Where the ego fools us, however, is in the falsity that we need to receive anything outside of ourselves. Everything we receive comes from the Light. The Light is Present and everywhere right now; within and among us. It is ready to give us everything we need; in fact It has already arranged for all our sustenance before our knowledge of perceived lack. But in order to build a trusting awareness in this reality we must have certainty that the illusion is indeed an illusion. The illusion that we have lack comes from the ego and not the Creator. Through our connection with the Creator sustenance flows easily.

How does one build a relationship with anything that is invisible to the five senses? How do we create a relationship with the Creator when our five senses cannot perceive the Creator's invisible Light? It happens through a steady connection to Wisdom, which is the residue of the Creator's creative handiwork that is among us. Through trust and certainty in what we know to be true, Light comes through us and we receive the understanding that The One exists. Our true nature then begins to channel Light into this world.

The world would have us believe that we have a lack of resources, whether that be food, money, love, etc. The reality is that there is no lack except our lack of receiving Light and then sharing what we receive with others. The lack is in our lack of understanding what our real nature is. This is the only lack this world really has. Our world has yet to understand that its sole purpose in creation is to become a vessel for Light. When we realize this on an individual and collective level the amount of provision and abundance everywhere will be astonishing. This is what we refer to as The Age of Meshiach or Messiah. "And the wise shall shine as the brightness of the firmament." (*Daniel 12:3*) The Kabbalistic text *The Zohar* states it another way. *The Zohar* states regarding this eventual global realization, "The brightness moves up and then down, shines throughout all aspects, is drawn and comes forth, and never ceases to shine. And the brightness procreates." (*Vayera 62, The Zohar*).

We are One and we will shine together as One. We now shine like the moon but a day will come when our reflection of Light will be analogous to the moon shining as bright as the sun. The brightness will come from a realization of what our true collective nature is, that being a collective channel for the Light of the Creator. There is nothing brighter than the fulfillment of Creation, which will eventually happen. It is the Creator's choice for us, and our choice for ourselves.

ABOUT THE AUTHOR

J ared Stuart is a bright and innovative, up and coming author who has the capacity to authentically communicate complex ideas in a simple and profound way. His insights into Wisdom and spirituality are inclusive, positive and uplifting. He has a capacity through writing and public speaking to connect with a broad audience, and to share his insights respectfully yet relevantly.

Jared has a Bachelor's in Religion and a Master's in Ministry from Pepperdine University in Malibu, CA. He has also spent the past decade studying Kabbalah. He innovatively merges spiritual teachings from Christianity and Kabbalah from a precise, refreshing and meditatively poetic perspective. There is a truthfulness in what Jared writes and says. His writings will challenge your own paradigms, and in the process allow you the opportunity to see life in a new way.

Jared resides in Los Angeles, CA and can be contacted through

bookofwisdom@earthlink.net.